Stafford
in old picture postcards

by
Roy Lewis
and
Joan Anslow

European Library – Zaltbommel/Netherlands

Second edition: 1994

GB ISBN 90 288 2786 2 / CIP

© 1984 European Library – Zaltbommel/Netherlands

No part of this book may be reproduced in any form, by print, photoprint, microfilm or any other means, without written permission from the publisher.

INTRODUCTION

Stafford was founded on an island of firm land with a loop of river on one side and low lying marsh on the other. This was the area that formed the mediaeval walled town. There was a north to south road on the only firm approaches to the town. On the north was Gaolgate and on the south Greengate and the Green Bridge. A causeway across the low ground led to Eastgate, the third gate in the town walls.

As the town's population grew, suburbs grew outside the Gaolgate (Foregate) and across the Green Bridge (Forebridge) but expansion in other directions was impossible. In the early-nineteenth century Foregate grew rapidly as new streets for shoe workers were built round the Marston Road. The railway came to Stafford in 1837 with a station on the far side of the river — there was no space elsewhere. In the mid-nineteenth century a whole suburb of Castletown grew up close to the station and largely inhabited by railway workers. This suburb was eventually linked more closely to the town by a new road — Victoria Road — and river bridge. Central, within-the-walls, Stafford in the second half of the nineteenth century remained an area with many half timbered buildings, and in the side lanes away from the main streets, there were chaotic small brick buildings and houses crowded on each other by lack of space. Photographs in the book illustrate both of these features.

This central area was in many ways unsavory. An assize judge in 1870 described it as 'the most stinking town I was ever in in my life'. A few years earlier Dickens had likened it to a Dodo — dead. In 1882 twelve samples of drinking water from various town wells were tested: only two were found fit for human consumption. Townspeople had built up an immunity to the smells and polluted water but strangers were often made ill within a few days.

The last quarter of the nineteenth century saw a determined effort to improve conditions in the town. A main drainage system was started in 1880; a piped water system from a pumping station at Milford began in 1890; the town's first sewage works, allowing privies to be replaced by water closets, opened in 1897. Low lying land along the river was drained and became Victoria Park.

At the same time other services came to Stafford. In 1892 the Public Brine Baths opened: in 1878 the Corporation bought the gas works and extended it and in 1895 started an electricity works. In 1887 the National Telephone Company Limited opened the first telephone exchange in Stafford. The cattle market was moved out of Gaolgate where it had become a source of bitter complaint because of smells as well as traffic hold ups. Other markets were also taken off the street.

New terraced brick houses, solidly built and having indoor water and sanitation began to be built. The first council houses were built at Broadeye in 1901. Even before this the enclosure of Coton Field had made new areas of land on the far side of the low lying land available for building. Corporation Street was laid out in the 1890's followed by part of Oxford Gardens. Corporation Street was extended by Riverway with another new bridge over the Sow in 1914. Lammascote and Coton Fields estates also date from this period. Yet another large estate was built by Siemens in the years after 1903 when it moved its electrical engineering works and many of its staff from Woolwich to Stafford.

The photographs in this book all date from 1890 until 1930. They show Stafford as it was during this period of rapid change. Some of the town of 1890 was, of course, demolished in the process, some with no regrets. Yet the best of the older Stafford was retained and a Staffordian of 1890 suddenly brought back in 1930 would have found many buildings which he recognised.

The largest single source of pictures of the town at this time is the picture postcard. These became popular soon after 1900 and millions were produced and sent each year. Cards of Stafford were printed by national companies such as Valentine, Tuck, Dennis and Boots, by W. Shaw of Burslem and by local businesses such as Dawson's and the Stafford branch of W.H. Smith's, as well as many smaller companies and shops. However, they have a limited variety. Each company produced cards of St. Mary's Church, the Market Square, the High House etc., but no one produced a card of Back Walls or Tenterbanks.

For this reason it has been necessary to supplement postcards with photographs. Our thanks must go to the many people who have loaned photographs for inclusion in this book.

Finally, there are already one or two books of photographs of Stafford as it was. Care has been taken to duplicate as few as possible of the photographs reproduced there.

Acknowledgements

The Authors would like to thank the following for their help, and for permission to reproduce these photographs:
A.E. Anslow: 69, 93
W. Clay: 46
Mrs. E. Dymott: 38
C. Ecclestone
H. Hill: 63
A. Leese: 91
R.A. Lewis: all postcards reproduced
Lotus Ltd: 89
Mrs. A. Middleton: 90
Mrs. M. Mitchell: 102
P. Newbold: 38
Mrs. Sherratt: 85
A. Sherratt: 92
Bertram Sinkinson O.B.E., hon. F.R.P.S.: 71, 80
Stafford Historical and Civic Society: 7, 11, 19, 21, 23, 25, 26, 35, 103
Museum of Staffordshire Life: 53
Staffordshire County Record Office: 40
Staffordshire Schools History Service
F.B. Stitt B.A., B. Litt., F.R. Hist. S.
Mrs. M. Turner
F. Warden
F. Waygood
The Trustees of the William Salt Library
Mrs. Woolhouse and Miss I. Woolhouse: 105

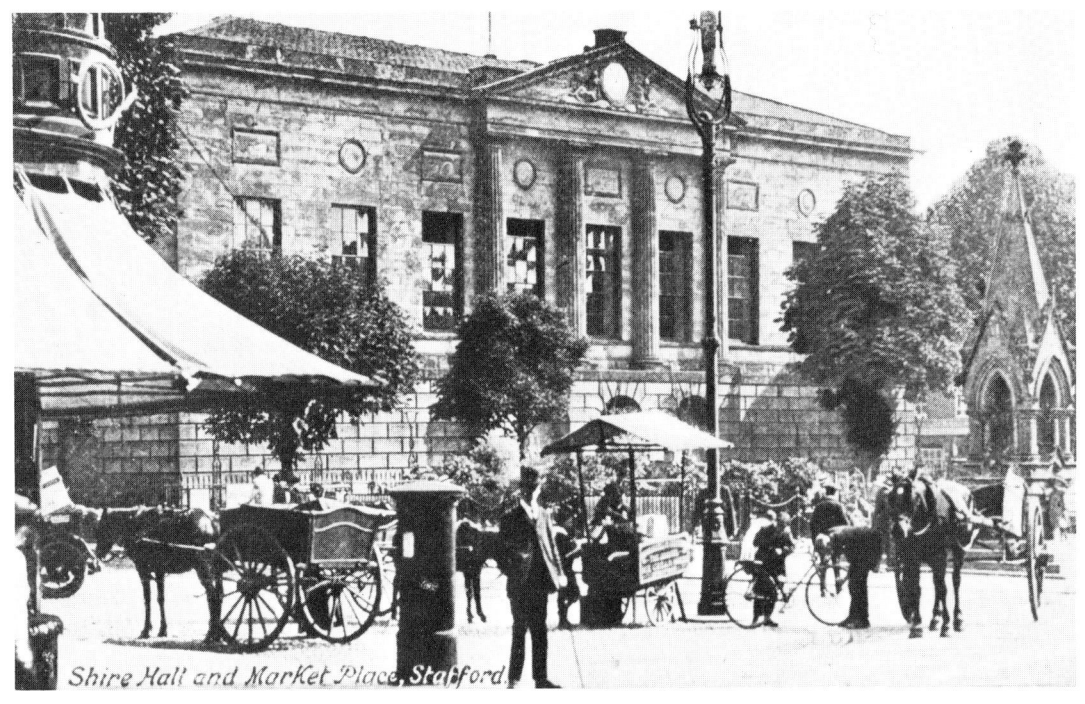

1. The Market Square is the centre of Stafford. Here royal visitors from James I to Edward VII were received. Here the town roasted two oxen at Queen Victoria's Diamond Jubilee and here the Suffragette Pilgrims' attempted to address the people of Stafford in 1913. This postcard of about 1914 shows the busy square with one of the town's Italian ice-cream vendors with his barrow packed with ice to keep the ice-cream cool. In the background is the Shire Hall built in the fashionable classical style of 1798. The Shire Hall was the meeting place for the County J.P.'s it was a court building for both Quarter Sessions and Assizes and it was also the social centre of the town in the early nineteenth century when fashionable balls were held in its great 75 feet long hall for the local gentry to show off their ladies.

MARKET SQUARE AND GUILDHALL, STAFFORD.

2. This view of Market Square was taken in the 1920's. It is dominated by the ornate drinking fountain erected in 1887 to mark Queen Victoria's Golden Jubilee. The space in front of Mummery's shop on the right had been a cab stand for the first horse-drawn cabs in the town and was, in the 1920's, still a stand for motor cabs. The building on the far left is the Guildhall built in 1854 for Borough Council meetings and to house the town's police station. The building also housed a large two wheeled stretcher used by the police to fetch bodies in cases of accident or murder. Old people remember seeing it pushed through the town with a blanket over the shape on the stretcher.

3. Stafford was first granted an annual fair in 1261 by Henry III. By 1900, a pleasure fair — (The Gorby Market) was held in the Market Square at the same time as cattle fairs in other streets of the town. The Gallopers were steam driven, the stalls in front of the swing boats probably sold ginger snaps, and other good things. A high-light in Stafford's year. One lady remembers that she always had a new pinafore for the Gorby Fair.

4. On Wednesday, 22nd June, 1897, the central feature of the celebrations for Queen Victoria's Jubilee was the roasting and eating of two oxen, presented to the town by G.E. and A.W. Meakin of Cresswell Hall. Two grates were built in the Market Square in front of the Shire Hall, the carcases secured on two spits, the fires lit about ten o'clock on Tuesday evening, and the meat was ready to eat by nine o'clock Wednesday morning. The huge crowds eagerly demanded a taste of the succulent meat, but by noon, the sun shone with such warmth that the little meat left was stinking, and every eatable morsel had vanished. Several local businessmen then donated sheep, and four were put on each spit, cooked by three o'clock, and all eaten by four o'clock. During the day beer had been available for tickets, donated by local brewers. The town of Stafford had never seen such a magnificent celebration, and probably never will again.

5. Queen Victoria's Jubilee Day in 1897 was fine and warm. A public procession led by the volunteer band, the Mayor, a body of police and many members paraded from the Market Square through the streets and back again. The ranks of the volunteers opened and they fired three rounds of blank ammunition, the National anthem was sung, a Royal salute and three hearty cheers for the Queen given. People watched from all vantage points, including the scaffolding where Mr. Brookfield was building his new shop on the corner of Market Square.

6. The Swan was the principal coaching inn of the town before the railway came to Stafford. A high arch between the second and third of the semi-circular bay windows led to stables and a smithy where horses were shod and wheels repaired. In 1852 Dickens visited Stafford and found the Swan fallen on lean times. He described it as the 'extinct town-inn, the Dodo'. He ordered sole for dinner and sat in the bay window watching 'Boots' cross the road to a fishmongers and return with something in a paper 'slapping his leg and pretending it is something else than my dinner... because the Dodo has nothing in the larder'. By the time this view was taken just after the 1914-1918 War the stables had become a garage but the fish shop can still be seen on the other side of Greengate Street.

7. 'Dales Old Shop' stood opposite the Swan Hotel in Greengate Street. It was supposedly the first house to be built in St. Chad's churchyard, about 1500. It was being used as an ironmonger's shop in 1811 and remained so until its demolition in the 1950's. It is remembered as having been dim and dark inside, crammed with fishing tackle, ironmongery, and carpentry tools, it was like an Aladdin's cave of wonders. Hanging from the centre gable could be seen a huge copper kettle, and sometimes a fishing rod with a large fish on the end.

8. The Manchester and Liverpool District Banking Company opened its Stafford branch in 1832, in Bank House, Greengate Street — the building on the extreme left, now the offices of an estate agent. The bank moved next door and eventually had the building with three gables designed and built on this site by the County Architect. It was a liberal mixture of architectural styles, which blended surprisingly well. The banking hall had huge open fireplaces at either end. It was demolished and replaced by a new bank building in the 1970's.

9. The Alexandra was built as a town house in the sixteenth century, on the corner of Tipping Street and Greengate Street. In the late-eighteenth century it was the home of Thomas Lovatt and his wife, who was the sister of William Horton 'The Father of Stafford's Shoe Trade'. It became a public house in the late-nineteenth century, and remained a hotel until its demolition in the early 1960's, when it was replaced by a supermarket.

ROYAL BRINE BATHS, STAFFORD.

10. The Brine Baths were built in 1892 to a design by Councillor George Wormald. As well as public baths there was a brine bath to which brine was pumped from a spring on Stafford Common. After a visit by the Duchess of Teck in 1895 the baths were known as the Royal Brine Baths. At the side of the baths was a landing stage where rowing boats could be hired. The boats belonged to Martin Mitchell who had a small cycle shop in the front of the Baths building but it was Old Joe, the boatman, who is remembered. He can be seen standing in one of the boats. The youths who hired boats were all a little afraid of him and there are many stories of him taking out a boat to hunt down those who failed to return within their allotted time.

11. These old buildings and boathouse were demolished in 1890 when the Brine Baths were built.

12. Until the Second World War all firemen in Stafford were volunteers. The Fire Station was next to the Brine Baths, and incorporated in the Baths buildings was the tall tower to dry the hoses and house the escape ladder. This photograph was taken in 1927, on the occasion of the opening of the David Hollin Nurses Home by Prince Henry, who later became Duke of Gloucester. Before 1914 fires were fought with hand operated pumps or a steam engine. Stafford bought its first motor engine in 1913, a Leyland with solid tyres.

13. When the new library building was opened in 1914, its roof provided a vantage point for local photographers. This view was taken for one of W.H. Smith's postcards just after the 1914-1918 War. The most noticeable feature of traffic in Bridge Street is the number of cyclists and the mixture of other traffic from the open topped double-decker bus on its way to Radford to the horse-drawn milk float. The motor bus is on the first regular route in the town and this is the only known picture showing one of these buses. The milk float is probably 'Milky' Wright who lived in Mill Street and kept his cows in a field where Jen shoes is today. After milking them twice a day he delivered milk from churns on his float.

14. Until 1914 the Borough Library was housed in the Borough Hall. In 1914 a grant from the Carnegie Trust made the new building shown here possible. Besides the library the building housed the Wragge collection of specimens collected abroad by Clement Wragge of Oakamoor. Even in 1914 a policeman was usually to be found on duty in the middle of this road junction.

15. In May 1928, the librarian of the Free Library arranged with the Local Education Authority to invite classes of children into the library in school hours, to talk to them and encourage them to use and enjoy books. This photograph was taken during one of these classes. In August of that year a new juvenile department was opened in the library. The Reading Room had children's periodicals, study tables and reference books to help with homework. Children were allowed to use the department on obtaining tickets on the recommendation of parents and teachers.

16. When the Staffordshire and Worcestershire Canal was opened in 1772, its nearest point to Stafford town was Radford Bridge where a wharf was built. Goods were unloaded here and brought into the town on a horse-drawn tramway. In 1816 a lock was made between the canal and the River Sow and the river itself deepened and straightened to allow canal narrowboats laden with coal to come up to the town. At Stafford, a coal wharf was built by digging a channel parallel to the river. This photograph shows the river on the right and the channel to the coal wharf on the left. A coal cart can just be seen far left. In the 1930's the extra channel was filled in. Tesco's store is now on the site.

17. Radford was where the road to Lichfield crossed the River Penk. In the late-eighteenth century it was also the place where the Staffordshire and Worcestershire Canal came nearest to Stafford and a canal bridge was built next to the river bridge. There was a small canal basin to the left of the road from which Stafford's first railway line carried goods into town until it closed down in 1814. The canal wharf where boats tied up led to a canalside public house – The Trumpet – on the right hand side of the road and various canal stores and warehouses on the left. With the decline of the canal the basin was filled in during the nineteenth century and the warehouses etc. demolished in 1972 to make way for Radford Marina, now also gone to make way for a garage.

18. Gaolgate Street is the north end of Stafford's main street. In this picture of about 1905 can be seen some of the town's crowded shop-windows. The Home and Colonial Store sold tea and other provisions, next door was Hazlewood's the drapers, then the King Edward VII public house, a china store, and the Maypole Dairy Company. The Maypole is remembered as 'a lovely shop; its walls were tiled with pictures of farms and dairy scenes. You could taste the cheese before you bought it, and butter was patted and stamped by the shopkeeper'. Until 1909 Gaolgate Street was known as Cow Street, as cattle sales were held in the street. The smell and the nuisance was considerable.

19. In 1887, fire destroyed four shops from the corner of Market Square round into Gaolgate Street, despite the valiant efforts of the Volunteer Fire Brigade's manual equipment. There was a lack of water. The council believed there to be ample water flowing beneath the streets, but this was not so, and the Asylum drain was empty also. The council opened a subscription list to buy a steam fire-engine as the hand pumps had not coped. Fortunately most of the shopkeepers were insured, but Stafford had lost Elizabethan House, and other timbered buildings. The photograph shows towns-people viewing the ruins the next morning.

20. In 1889 the iron pillar drinking fountain in Gaol Square was erected by the widow of Thomas Sidney to the memory of her husband, a local Grammar School boy who became Lord Mayor of London, 1853/54. The shaft of the fountain supported two lamps, and originally had a figure of Hercules at the top. Hercules was later replaced by the lamp as on this postcard.

21. On the 8th May, 1928, a motor van backed into the Sidney Fountain and the whole structure tumbled down. The lamp on top had been replaced by a clock in 1916. Behind the smash can be seen the Hairdressing Saloon, and on the corner of Mount Street, Bigham's dress shop. A Jenkinson's van is parked by the shops. This area has now entirely disappeared under new road schemes.

22. The north end of Eastgate Street was part of the town markets until late in the nineteenth century. The Borough Hall is on the site of the old pig market, the area in the foreground of this picture was for many years the horse fair and just off the picture is Pitcher Bank, the site of the crockery market. The house with the trees in front is Eastgate House which was built by General John Dolphin in 1683. Dolphin later became M.P. for Stafford. In the eighteenth century the old front was replaced by the one seen in the picture. In 1839 it became the home of T.B. Elley, one of the principal shoe manufacturers and leather tanners in the town. In 1891 it was bought by the County Council at first as the Chief Constable's house and more recently as the Registry Office.

23. Sheridan and Fox while being of the same political persuasion, were also very good friends, therefore it was appropriate that neighbouring Inns in Eastgate Street should be called the Sheridan and the Fox and George. In this photograph of 1904 the Fox and George is empty awaiting demolition. It was replaced by a grocer's shop. A few doors away, at 6, Eastgate Street, Sheridan once had his Committee Rooms, and addressed the voters from an upstairs window.

24. The Borough Hall was built in Eastgate Street in 1876, at a cost of £11,000. It was designed in the French Gothic style of the fourteenth century. Originally it combined accommodation for the Borough Council offices on the ground floor, and on the first floor, a large hall for meetings, concerts, plays and dances. Still in use in 1984, the Council have moved to new premises, but a renovated theatre, bars and restaurant complex serves the people of Stafford.

25. On 13th January, 1906, there was a General Election. In Stafford the Candidates were C.E. Shaw (Liberal) and S.R.C. Bosanquet (Conservative). Everyone wore either a green favour for Liberal, or a blue favour for Conservative. Shaw was the retiring member and his Committee Rooms, shown here, were next to the Wheatsheaf Inn in Gaolgate Street. For perhaps the first time motor-cars played a big part in an election. Shaw had more cars lent to him than Bosanquet who, however, had plenty of horse-drawn vehicles. Sixty extra police were drafted into the town, but were fortunately not needed. The result announced at 9.30 p.m. to the throng was Shaw, Liberal 1,947 votes, Bosanquet, Conservative 1,636. Children roamed the streets chanting support for a particular candidate, one song was:

Vote, Vote, Vote for Mr. Shaw, Boys,
For he is sure to win the day,
For Mr. Shaw's a man,
And we'll have him if we can,
If you'll only put your shoulder to the wheel.

26. Stafford was surrounded by walls on three sides, and the river and an embankment on the fourth. There were three gates in the walls, the main one was the Greengate, on the south of the town. In 1928, Mercer's shop, on the corner of Millbank, was demolished for road widening. The remnants of the south west wing of the Greengate were found, and part of the old wall, extending 50 yards towards the Coach and Horses Public House. Unfortunately most of the wall was covered again when the new road was made. This photograph appeared in the Staffordshire Advertiser and shows part of the old town wall and the lower courses of a later brickwall.

27. The old chocolate shop was at the Lammascote end of North Walls in the 1920's. Part of the old town wall is clearly seen on the right. It was near this spot where the East Gate would have been, joining Back Walls North and Back Walls South (now North Walls and South Walls). The remaining length of town wall still to be seen in this area has been moved from its original site and rebuilt. Note the advertisement for Lifebuoy soap, and Crawford's crackers.

28. Celia Fiennes, travelling through Stafford in the late-seventeenth century, wrote that 'Its an old built town, timber and plaister pretty much, in long peaked roofs of tiling'. This is a remnant of that wealth of timbered houses, and was situated in South Walls. Many of the larger timbered buildings can be seen elsewhere in this book.

29. The windmill in Broadeye was built in 1796, partly from stone from the Elizabethan Town Hall demolished about this time. A carving of the Royal Arms from the Hall was placed over the doorway. Steam power was used by 1847, and by this time the old sails had been removed and the top altered so that it could no longer turn into the wind. By the 1880's the building was no longer used as a mill. It became in turn a grain store and a shop. The cottages were tiny and damp, two steps led from the street into a living room.

30. Cherry Street was originally called Talbot Lane. The half demolished building on the corner was a tea room. The cottages were very old, and this area of Cherry Street disappeared when the Technical College was built. There was a dairy here in the late-nineteenth century, which kept cows in a yard, people could buy ½d. worth of milk. The dairyman delivered milk with a yoke across his shoulders supporting two large cans.

31. These little cottages stood in St. Chad's Place, behind St. Chad's Church. They date from the days when everyone lived right in the town, in and around the shops. The cottages were probably two up, two down, workers' housing. Also in St. Chad's Place was Jen's Shoe Factors who provided materials to outworker shoemakers to make up in their own homes. The outworkers would collect their leather on Monday mornings, and then return the made-up shoes the following week and receive their payment. Those shoemakers were called 'snobs', they wore frock coats and top hats, were fiercely independent, and comparatively well-off.

32. Stafford Street was formerly known as Jerningham's Row. Many years ago the shop on the corner was noted for making 'Stafford Wiggs'. These were three cornered buns with carraway seeds, sugar baked onto the top, then buttered before eating. The cakes were supposedly introduced into England from France, and originally called 'Wygges'.

33. Queen Elizabeth I progressed through Crabbery Street (then named Crowberrie Lane) in 1597 on her way to visit Stafford Castle. On the left of this postcard of about 1905 can be seen the Albert Hall, a theatre and later a picture house. Further down on the left is the Penny Bazaar. The shopfronts, and upper windows on the right hand side have remained much the same to this day.

34. Salter Street is one of the old streets of Stafford, it is mentioned as Salters Lane in the late-fourteenth century. The Vine Inn was there by 1782, and the street became known as Vine Street. Despite being named 'Salter Street' officially in 1838, it is still known locally as Vine Street in 1984.

35. This old public house was in North Walls; its sign should read Maltsters Arms (not Malsters Arms), but it was known locally as the 'Hole in the Wall'. It brewed its own beer on the premises. In the distance on the right can be seen the old Grammar School building of the early-nineteenth century, which, by 1905, was being used as a warehouse. North Walls follows the line of the old town walls, and behind them ran Thieves Ditch, a repository for rubbish and refuse.

36. The Noah's Ark on the corner of Crabbery Street is, perhaps, the oldest building in Stafford. It would have been old when Queen Elizabeth I stopped here for a glass of wine before riding on to Stafford Castle in 1575. Under the projecting porch on the right was a way through to a courtyard with an old tree in the centre. It must have once been the home of a wealthy Stafford family. In 1831 it was occupied by George Keeling, a currier, and owned by Colonel William Brookes. Soon afterwards it became a public house called the Noah's Ark. In 1877 it was bought by the Corporation who took it down in part and demolished the overhanging porch as part of a road widening scheme. The original stone was reused in the alterations. But why was it called Noah's Ark?

37. This house on the corner of Bath Street has a strange history of murder. In 1831 it became the home of Colonel William Brookes, a bachelor and a retired East Indian Company Officer. Brookes had an illegitimate daughter, Anne, by his housekeeper Mary Thornton. Mary had a sharp temper, behaved in most unladylike ways and even struck the Colonel, who did not dare turn her out because he doted on his daughter, Anne. Anne was sent off to a finishing school at Great Haywood. The Colonel died leaving Anne a heiress but with the rents of most of the property left to Mary Thornton for life. Anne was courted by a poor young doctor and they married. The doctor gambled and lived beyond his means and, when Mary Thornton came to stay with her daughter, she was suddenly taken ill. Within a fortnight she was dead and Colonel Brookes' property was inherited by Anne. The doctor's name was William Palmer of Rugeley and Mary Thornton was the first of several victims to die by poison. Five years later Anne also died mysteriously. Palmer, convicted of murder, was hung outside Stafford Gaol.

38. The Sun Inn is in Lichfield Road. The ostler standing in the gateway worked there for thirty years. He took care of the horses when customers came in their traps and carts. He also looked after bicycles left there, charging 2d. a time. At other times he helped in the bar. Behind the Inn was the Sun smithfield, where cattle sales were held.

39. The Jolly Crafts stood at the corner of Chapel Street and Stafford Street. Stafford was a market town and on market days, the nearby villagers came in to do their shopping and have a day out. They often travelled in a pony and trap or other horse-drawn vehicles. The Jolly Crafts had room for six horses with two separate stalls at each end, and the country people could stable their horses there while they shopped.

40. 'The Old Blue Posts' was in Martin Street, a public house much used by the actors and actresses from the nearby Lyceum Theatre. Sometimes the Thespians boarded here, and could not always pay. One actress left a ruby ring in lieu of her keep, and the descendant of the landlord still has it. The Inn was demolished in 1893 to make room for the County Buildings which now occupy the whole of Martin Street.

"PETER"
AWARDED A "DAILY MIRROR" GUGNUNC COLLAR FOR BRAVERY

41. Peter belonged to William Jones, licensee of the Crown Inn, Queensville. In 1928 he pulled an eight year old boy out of the River Sow and saved him from drowning. The Daily Mirror awarded the dog a Gugnunc collar for bravery. (Those of you who remember Pip, Squeak and Wilfred may be able to translate gugnunc from the special language they used.) In later years Peter appeared at many dog shows and paraded as the dog V.C. This postcard was published by the Daily Mirror to raise money for charity.

GENERAL POST OFFICE, STAFFORD. 1910.

42. The Post Office moved from Eastgate Street to this building in Market Square on the corner of Bank Passage in 1867, and remained here until 1914 when it moved to its present site in Greengate Street. In those days there were four deliveries a day in Stafford starting at 7.00 a.m., 11.20 a.m., 2.20 p.m. and 5.20 p.m. The Post Office was open from 8.00 a.m. to 8.00 p.m. for most business and for telegraphic business from 7.30 a.m. to 9.00 p.m. The branch Post Office at the railway station was even open from 8.00 a.m. to 10.00 a.m. on Sundays, Good Friday and Christmas Day.

43. Chetwynd House was built in 1740 by William Chetwynd. The Duke of Cumberland stayed there on his return from suppressing the Scottish Rebellion in 1745. Richard Brinsley Sheridan, while M.P. for Stafford, often visited Chetwynd House when William Horton lived there in the early-nineteenth century. The railings are of very fine French workmanship, they were presented by Louis Phillipe of France to Earl Ferrars, then English Ambassador in Paris. The earl presented them to Dr. Knight who lived in Chetwynd House. In 1914 the house became Stafford's General Post Office. The scene shown here is the grand opening on the 4th April.

Series of the S. P. T. and P. P. C. Coy., Glasgow.

25 GREENGATE, STAFFORD.

44. Goodall's on the corner of Greengate Street and Back Walls South was typical of town centre grocery shops before the 1914-1918 War. Inside were polished wood counters where the ladies of Stafford were offered chairs while they gave the assistants their orders which would later in the day be taken round to their house in the horse-drawn trap on the right of this picture. None of the goods were sold in packets — assistants had to weigh out sugar, rice, currants, raisins, sago and tapioca. Treacle and black syrup were kept in large barrels and ladled out into jars as necessary. Tea in plywood chests came by train and was delivered to the shop where the owner mixed his own 'Goodall's tea' from the chests stored in the shop.

45. Brookfields, said to have been established in 1743, was a large department store on the corner of Market Square and Greengate Street. It sold almost everything, from furniture to clothing, china and glassware, trunks, it even had a funeral department and a removal business. This photograph shows the millinary department about 1905. The hats in vogue then were very large, and often extravagantly trimmed.

46. H.J. Clay's pork butcher's shop was in the Foregate. This photograph of Christmastime 1914 shows the sides of pork on display outside the shop, and even hung across the window of the house on the left hand side. The notice on the window states 'all goods manufactured on the premises', this would mean sausages, pork pies and bacon.

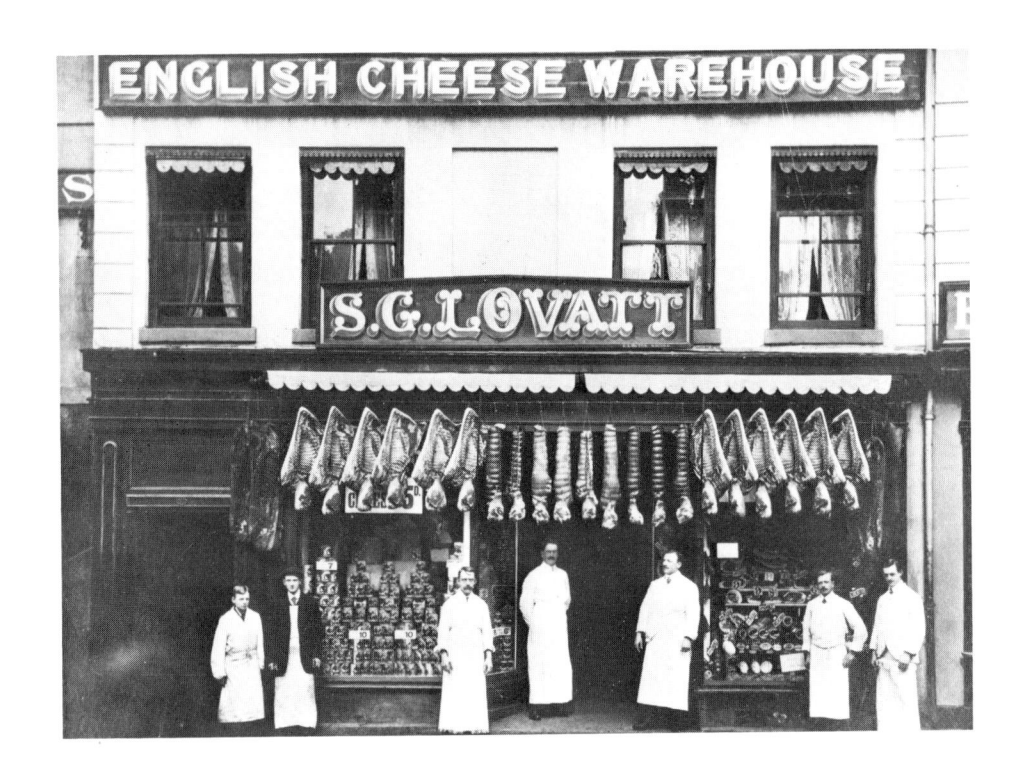

47. Lovatt's shop was in Gaolgate Street. The crowded window displays everything sold, with clear price tickets. The shop specialised in cheeses, but obviously sold tinned goods, bacon, and other groceries besides. The shop assistants are all male in their spotless aprons. The curtains at the windows show that the upstairs was used as living accommodation, as was the case in most Stafford shops.

48. The northern suburbs of Stafford in the nineteenth century were the centre of the shoemaking industry. The house on the left of this picture is just one of many centres of this industry. In 1818 a trade directory lists 'William Elley, shoe manufacturer, Foregate'. This was his house. In the garden behind the house was his warehouse where he stored leather, had it cut to the required shape and put it out to shoemakers who made up the shoes in their own houses before returning them for payment to the warehouse. In the distance on the right can just be seen Bebbington's baker's shop, built on the site of the old Franciscan Friary, where bakers working late often heard the ghosts of mediaeval friars, — or claimed they did.

49. Marston Road is a typical example of nineteenth century urban growth. The terraced housing is interspersed by small shops and public houses. Built to accommodate workers in the growing shoe industry in the north end of Stafford, the area became a complete working-class community with its own churches and schools.

50. In October 1765 a meeting of Staffordshire gentlemen agreed to subscribe money to open an Infirmary in Stafford. Within a few days a house was taken on lease in the Foregate and the Infirmary established. Other houses in the Foregate were added, but by 1768 it was obvious that a larger building, planned as an Infirmary, was required. This was opened in 1772. In 1820 the first operating theatre was built here and in the Board Room was preserved a copper vessel in which an arsenical paste was kept to spread round the incisions made by surgeons. This was an early attempt at antiseptic surgery. In 1896 the Infirmary was much altered and given a new front. This photograph shows the men's surgical ward, one of those created in 1896.

51. A town pageant was held each year to raise funds for Stafford Infirmary. Decorated floats would compete for cups, and there were prizes for the best decorated street; a pageant queen was chosen, and a grand parade wound its way through the town, collecting money from the watching crowds, until it reached the Common. Here a fair would be in full swing. This photograph shows one of the entries, Jack People's Miniature Fair, about 1911.

52. Stafford Gaol was built in 1793 with towers at intervals along its walls. One of these can be seen in the distance in this picture. The main prison wall had outside it another wall of brick about 6 feet high which was supposed to prevent those outside putting ladders against the main wall. On top of the gatehouse seen here, a scaffold was erected whenever a prisoner was to be hung. In 1817 this collapsed and from that time a huge box on wheels was used. This would just go through the nearer gate and on it the gallows were erected. On these gallows Palmer, the Rugeley poisoner, was hung in front of vast crowds. The last public hanging here took place in 1866. Today the towers have gone, after being used as council houses for a time; the outer brick wall is taken away leaving a very wide pavement, and the gatehouse has been rebuilt.

53. Male prisoners in Stafford Gaol sentenced to hard labour might be set to work stone breaking or on the crank or on the treadmill. The treadmills, which were a long drum with steps fixed at eight or ten inch intervals, ground corn or pumped up water. Prisoners were marched to the tread mill and at the word of command began walking up this 'endless ladder' while hanging on to a small chain with a handle. If the man did not catch every step that came round, his toes were crushed. He worked for 16 minutes with up to 50 steps a minute and then rested for 8 minutes. This went on for eight hours each day. It was the most feared of prison work. This photograph was taken inside Stafford Gaol about 1870 and is one of a series taken by Flamanc and now in the Museum of Staffordshire Life at Shugborough.

54. On top of the Norman motte, there had been a mediaeval stone keep. This was destroyed in the Civil War. In the early-nineteenth century William Jerningham cleared away the rubble to expose the old foundations and his son, Edward, started to rebuild the Castle 'in the style of Edward III'. Two towers and walls and rooms at one end of the building were completed — the rest was never finished. Edward Jerningham died in 1849 and after that no one lived here except a caretaker who would show people round for a small fee. Many older people remember being shown round the Castle and being sold pop and biscuits. It was a popular place for a weekend walk as can be seen in this picture taken about 1904 showing the rebuilt towers and the unfinished walls behind them.

55. This postcard is titled Castle Road, today it would be Newport Road. The area shown was also called Deanshill because a farm just off this road on the left had been granted to the church of St. Mary in Stafford before the Norman Conquest. In the middle of the nineteenth century the owner of Deanshill Farm was John Painter who was a noted race horse breeder and trainer. His stables were approximately where the road in this picture bends to the right and the gallops for his horses on the higher ground to the left of the road where the present golf course lies. William Palmer, the Rugeley poisoner, was a close friend of John Painter and, when arrested, was negotiating to buy a house in Newport Road to be near the racing stables.

56. This house is Upmeads on the Newport Road, so called from the view across lawns and fields which no longer exists. The house, in spite of its appearance, dates from 1908 and is the earliest flat roofed house in England remaining as it was built. It was designed by the architect Edgar Wood, and is notable for being laid out symmetrically but on the garden side the windows have been deliberately planned so that the left half is different to the right.

57. David Hollin was born in 1844, the son of a railway guard. His father moved to Stafford soon after he was born. David, after working as a messenger boy at a newspaper office, was apprenticed as a clicker to a local shoemaker. At the age of 21 he set up his own shoemaking business in partnership with Zachariah Anderson, at first in premises behind Chetwynd House and later in a factory he designed himself in Rowley Street. About 1880 he built himself a luxurious house, called Highfield Manor, on the Newport Road. The gardens were said to be modelled on those of Versailles. In 1904 he had an album of photographs taken of his house and gardens. This is one of the photographs and shows Mr. and Mrs. Hollin and their niece at Highfield Manor.

58. A corn mill has existed on this site since the Middle Ages and perhaps earlier. This building had on it a date stone just below the top storey windows with 'G.B. 1834'. G.B. stood for George Brewster, miller. The mill was water powered and the river dammed up so that water could be led down chutes to drive the two water-wheels. One under the low arch on the right of the main mill building, the other under the taller arch on the right of the lower building. Because the river was dammed up, whenever there was heavy rain the low ground up river flooded. In 1876 the Corporation bought the mill and lowered the dam so that the water level was lower and flooding less. In 1957 the mill was demolished but the mill-wheels left as a reminder of the town mill.

59. When the Borough Council bought the town mill as part of a flood control scheme, they also found themselves the owners of a stretch of low lying land between the river and the station. In 1908 this land was opened as the Victoria Pleasure Grounds. It included a bandstand where concerts were given most summer weekends. In 1910, to mark the Coronation of King George V, a new area of park with a bowling green was laid out on the other side of the river and in 1911 the Coronation Bridge, seen on this postcard, was built to link the two parts of the park.

60. The Grand Junction Railway through Stafford was opened in 1837 with no official celebration, partly because the King had died a few days earlier and partly from a fear of accidents if a large crowd gathered. Nevertheless the Mayor organised an unofficial 21 gun salute for the first train. Stafford grew in importance as lines to Wellington were opened in 1849 and to Lichfield and Rugby in 1847. A whole railway suburb, Castletown, grew up for those who worked on the railways. In 1862 a new station was built by the railway company's architect, W. Baker, in an Italian style, with a cast iron framed canopy under which carriages could set down passengers under shelter. A new road to the station was opened in 1866 and in the same year the North Western Hotel was completed opposite the station. The station shown here was demolished in 1962 and the North Western Hotel in 1972.

61. When the Grand Junction Railway reached Stafford, its station was built on the opposite side of the river to the town centre and separated from it by low lying land along the river bank. The only approach to the station was by a road which branched off the Newport Road and formed a rather roundabout route from the town centre. A new and more direct road, Victoria Road, was opened in 1866 with a new bridge across the river. The building in the left foreground is the studio of C.E. Fowke, one of the leading photographers in Stafford in the early-twentieth century. He supplied postcard publishers with many of the photographs they needed and several photographs reproduced in this book are probably his.

62. On 12th March, 1906, the London and North Western Railway express from London to the North about to run into Stafford Station had to cross from one line to another on the south side of Newport Road Bridge. The engine and the first six coaches ran into the station safely, but the seventh coach left the rails and caused the three following coaches to be derailed. One coach was damaged on the bridge, the next was wrecked on some stables by the bridge, the brake van mounted the wreckage and the fourth van partially telescoped. Despite this terrible damage, only four people were injured and none of them badly. No explanation could be given for the derailment.

63. Queensville Stores was run for fifty years by Mr. T. Hill, seen here in front of his shop. Besides selling from his shop Mr. Hill took a horse and cart round the houses selling goods and vegetables, and buying rabbits from farmers, even fetching loads of coal from Littleton Colliery. The shop was on the very edge of Stafford, almost in the country, and had tie-ups for seven cows, two loose boxes, two pig sties, a cart shed and a huge garden. It also had its own bakehouse.

LICHFIELD ROAD, STAFFORD.

64. This postcard was published by William Shaw of Burslem about 1910. The photograph shows the old Lichfield Road on the right and on the left the newer road rising to cross the railway by a bridge.

65. It is difficult to recognise this postcard of the Lichfield Road. The old thatched cottages on the left have long been demolished to make way for a garage. The imitation Tudor three-storied building still stands but with shop-fronts inserted on the ground floor. Beyond that there has been extensive demolition for the traffic island at the end of the ring road but the distant spire of the Baptist Church can still be identified.

66. Silkmore was mentioned in Domesday as 'Selchemore'. In 1629 Thomas Chamberlin owned Silkmore Meadow and, when he died, he left £2 a year to Castle Church, £1.13s.4d. for the poor and 6s.8d. for a sermon to be preached on the Sunday after St. Andrew's day. By the late-eighteenth century Thomas Mottershaw owned the land and carried on with the charity. He probably built Silkmore Hall, replacing a much older building. A new garden front, staircase and hall were added in 1820, and by 1834 Thomas Hartshorn was the owner. The Hall, seen here in the 1920's, was demolished in the early 1960's, and has been replaced by a community of flats and bungalows for old people.

67. This country lane is unrecognisable to present day inhabitants of Stafford. It shows Silkmore Lane about 1905 with the fields and meadows of Silkmore Farm on the left and the lodge to Silkmore Hall on the right. Today Meadow Road is on the left where the field gate is in the picture and Hall Close on the right. In 1926 British Reinforced Concrete Engineering Co., Ltd. bought Silkmore Farm and built their factory there. This was followed by private building along Silkmore Lane before 1939 and in the 1950's by council estates at Meadow Road, Exeter Street and Sidney Avenue.

68. Reputed to be the longest street in Stafford, Corporation Street was built in the mid 1890's. It was known locally at the time as 'Clembelly Avenue' because it was said to be so smart and expensive that if you lived there you could not afford to eat.

69. The Staffordshire General Lunatic Asylum was built in 1818 for patients of all social classes. However, it became an asylum for paupers when Coton Hill Mental Hospital for private patients was built in 1854. Coton Hill stood in 30 acres and had its own farm which supplied the hospital with fresh milk, eggs, poultry etc. In the beautiful grounds was a private chapel, where services were held regularly. The patients could play tennis on the hospital courts, attend dances and films in the recreation hall, or play billiards in a well equipped billiard room. Coton Hill was demolished in 1976, except for the chapel, to make way for Stafford's new general hospital. This photograph shows Coton Hill in the 1920's.

70. Corporation Street School was built in 1895 by the Stafford School Board to replace the old British School in Earl Street. On the first day it opened so many pupils presented themselves that not all could be admitted. As numbers grew a separate block for infants was built (1900) and a new block for boys (1909) leaving the girls in the original building. Its first headmaster was John Wheeldon and in recent years the school has been renamed after him. The building was damaged by subsidence in the years after the Second World War and remodelled without a tower.

71. This school group from St. Paul's Church of England Elementary School was taken about 1905. Note the boys' stiff, shiny collars that could be sponged clean, the smaller boys are wearing the popular sailor collar, and all the boys wear knee breeches and long woollen socks. The girls are wearing heavy, fussy dresses, kept clean by the starched frilled white pinafores. All the children are wearing the same kind of strong, heavy hardwearing boots. These children left school at 14. If they passed the Labour Certificate they could leave at 13.

72. In 1928 the old Grammar School of King Edward VI received a major extension with the opening of the new wing along Friars Terrace. This extension provided space for much needed science laboratories — physics and chemistry in the new wing and biology in the old building. This photograph was taken soon after the new laboratories were opened. It shows the most up-to-date furniture and equipment for a school biology laboratory in 1928. Notice the different orders of animals and insects painted on the wall and the animal heads. These survived in school until at least 1940 but we have failed to find any information about their final fate.

73. Practical lessons for boys and girls were encouraged in Staffordshire Elementary Schools after the 1902 Education Act. The usual subjects were cookery, needlework, gardening and woodwork. By 1914 some 18 Elementary Schools in the county had courses which started with cardboard modelling and led on to light woodwork. This was done in an ordinary classroom. The county had also begun to train existing teachers to teach woodwork and soon there was a single woodwork bench in many classrooms. In post-war years woodwork centres with a specialist teacher, benches and tools were set up in a few places and the oldest boys from schools in the area spent half a day a week at these centres. This photograph shows the woodwork centre at Corporation Street School in Stafford in the late 1920's.

74. St. Mary's was a Royal Free Chapel before the Norman Conquest and as late as 1929 the Rector claimed that for this reason the Bishop of Lichfield had no authority over him or his church. The building shown in this postcard is a mixture of genuine mediaeval stonework and restoration by Gilbert Scott in 1841-1844 in what he thought might have been the original style of the church. The tower was once surmounted by a spire but as early as 1593 this collapsed bringing down with it part of the choir roof. The grave-stones in the foreground were moved and the whole churchyard levelled and grassed as a memorial to Stafford men and women killed in the Second World War.

Stafford. The Old College

75. These almshouses for six old men and six old women over 50 years old and born in Stafford or living there for 15 years were built about 1660 by Sir Martin Noell, a London merchant who came from Stafford. One was to be a matronly woman able to look after anyone who was sick and another an aged clergyman able to pray daily with the old people in the chapel on the left of the picture above. Noell died of the plague in London in 1665. The almshouses – often called the Old College – remained much as they were built until the 1960's.

76. A society of Wesleyan Methodists was formed in Stafford in 1783. After meeting for a time in a disused stable, described by Wesley as 'a deplorable hole', and in Cherry Street, the site of this chapel in Chapel Street was bought in 1811. The first chapel was pulled down in 1863 and the one shown in the photograph was built on the same site to a design by Hayley & Sons of Manchester. In 1984 plans exist to demolish all the church, except the tower, as part of a new market development.

77. Zion Chapel was built in Martin Street in 1810, a small building with a garden in front. When the Infirmary was altered (probably in 1896), the chapel bought the pillared portico, extended the chapel building over the garden right to the street, and put up a new façade more suited to the elegant portico they had bought.

St. Thomas' Church, Stafford.

78. Castletown was a suburb of houses built in the 1850's close to the Railway Station, to house the many railway servants coming to work in Stafford. St. Thomas' Church, built in 1866 was known as the railwaymen's church. The first incumbent, William Kendall, was a fine speaker, who attracted crowds to his sermons until he protested that the church was intended for the working-classes, and that fine silks and satins with extensive crinolines were a bar to ordinary people in more ways than one. St. Thomas' served the community until 1972 when a replacement church was built in Doxey, and the old building demolished.

Christ Church, Stafford.

79. After the enclosure of most of the common land to the north of Stafford in 1800, the area was rapidly built up to provide working-class houses for those engaged in the shoe trade, most of whom worked in their own homes. The growing population of the area led to the building of Christ Church in 1839, designed by George Hamilton in a mixture of Norman and Early English styles. There was a graveyard close by, where burials took place until 1873, and a National School which was older than the church. In recent years the church was closed because of falling attendances and the need for urgent repairs. It was demolished in 1983.

80. When the First World War came to an end at eleven o'clock on the 11th November, 1918, Stafford had a day of spontaneous celebration, schools and factories closed and crowds thronged the streets. The official Peace celebrations were held on 19th July, 1919. School children marched to the Common, each carrying a flag, there they were entertained with Punch and Judy shows, other entertainments, and refreshments. St. Mary's bells were rung and fireworks let off. A concert was held in Victoria Park and a special breakfast provided for the old folk. Headed by the Regimental Band the 3rd Battalion Bedfordshire Regiment marched to the Market Square, and can be seen here being welcomed by the Mayor. Then the soldiers marched to Lammascotes for a special dinner.

81. In the First World War 584 Stafford men died. In their memory the memorial in Victoria Square was erected in 1922, and a bed endowed in Stafford Infirmary. In November 1922, the memorial was unveiled by an ex-serviceman, Corporal Sturland, who had served in the Royal Field Artillery from 1915. He was badly wounded at Ypres and lost a leg. The bronze soldier on the plinth was equipped as if he had just left the trenches. His face looked haggard, worn and tired. He was holding his helmet in his right hand, as though he were crying: 'Hurrah, thank God the great task is accomplished.'

82. In 1883, there was a beerhouse in Telegraph Street called 'The Telegraph', it was kept by a Mrs. Bough. The name was most likely derived from the Railway Telegraph, owing to the beerhouse's proximity to the railway. In 1904 Sieman's works built an estate of houses nearby for its workers. Eley's Stafford Brewery soon afterwards rebuilt the Telegraph Inn, seen here, to serve the people of 'Sieman's colony'. Note the stacked barrels of beer, just delivered. This was probably the last public house built by Eley's to sell their own beer.

SALT AVENUE, STAFFORD.

83. Siemens Brothers transferred their heavy electrical equipment business from Woolwich to Stafford in 1900. 800 workers and their families moved to Stafford and caused an acute housing shortage. Siemens themselves built 88 houses in Siemens Road, Sabine Street, Lawrence Street and Salt Avenue. These varied from two-storied flats let for seven shillings a week to these larger houses in Salt Avenue built for their foremen. St. Leonard's School was also built largely to accommodate the children of Siemens workers. Siemens became part of English Electric in 1920.

Siemens Bros Dynamo Works, Stafford.

84. The German Siemens Brothers founded a heavy electrical equipment business at Woolwich. This flourished and a new, larger site became necessary. In 1900 they bought the Hough Estate off the Lichfield Road, attracted by the good road and railway links from Stafford. By 1903 the new factory in Stafford was making all kinds of electrical machinery. The wages of a skilled workman were 39 shillings a week for 52 hours. This was well-paid work and about 800 workmen and their families moved into Stafford from Woolwich. The factory was soon the largest single employer of labour in Stafford. In 1906 the name was changed to Siemens Brothers Dynamo Works and the German connections of the firm steadily reduced so that in 1914 there was no difficulty in the factory turning over to war work.

85. By 1916, women had taken over many of the jobs left vacant by the men at the front. Women were in the police, on the docks, on the land, were post girls and factory workers. These women war workers made munitions at Siemens and wore khaki mob caps and smocks. This photograph was taken at the annual hospital pageant. The words on the banner struck a patriotic note and made a powerful appeal to the crowds. The Prime Minister on more than one occasion publicly testified to the splendid war service of women, but it was pointed out that they were still not considered worthy of the vote, their service was desired and valued but not their intelligent co-operation.

86. These five 0-6-2 type tank locomotives were manufactured in 1928 by W.G. Bagnall Limited for the Federated Malay States. They were shipped whole, instead of being dismantled and packed into boxes, and a special lifting beam had to be made to lift the locomotives on board the train. They could not travel on their own wheels because they were made for metre gauge, not 4 foot 8½ inches as in England. Each locomotive, weighing 25 tons, was loaded on to well trolleys and was only just within the limits of rail transit.

87. In 1875 W.G. Bagnall, a Staffordian, who had had engineering training at his uncle's iron foundry in Wolverhampton bought a millwright's business in Castletown. In 1876 he built his first locomotive at the Castle Engine Works and over the next 85 years almost 2,000 locomotives were built here. Many of these were ordered by railways abroad and others by all the main railway companies of Britain. Later the firm fitted locomotives with Dormans diesel engines and in 1959 the business was sold to Dormans. This photograph shows the smith's shop or forge. The connecting rod in the drop hammer is for a GWR pannier tank. Notice the works 1'6" gauge narrow gauge railway system to the left of the old ex-mainline locomotive type boilers used for steam hammers.

CLICKING ROOM
MESSRS. E. BOSTOCK & Co., LTD.
LOTUS SHOE FACTORY, STAFFORD.

88. Bostock's shoe factory was built in Sandon Road in 1902, after the old factory in Glover Street burned down. It was very modern at the time, and people enjoyed the pleasant working conditions. This is a view of the clicking room. Skilled workers called 'clickers' laid out patterns of the different parts of a shoe on to pieces of leather and cut them out. The skill lay in being able to cut the pieces economically while allowing for the leather to 'stretch' the correct way for each shoe part. Bostocks had the reputation of making the best shoes in the country.

89. This view of the Lotus factory in the 1920's shows the girls in the closing room. Here the uppers were assembled, cemented together and machined. Then any eyelets, buttons and buttonholes were affixed, before the uppers were forwarded to the making room to await soles, insoles, stiffeners etc.

90. In 1893 Stafford's first Salt Works were set up near the Common Station. The brine was heated in large pans and the salt drawn off to the side. The salt was put into wooden blocks and dried in a hot house. The 'lumps' of salt were cut into smaller ones and eventually sold in the shops in 2 lb blocks. About 1913 magnesium was being added to salt, to make it free running. These young ladies are scooping the salt into packets, fastening the top and pasting on a brand label. For this they earned 3½d. per gross of packets.

91. This view of the ironing room of Stafford Steam Laundry was taken about 1905. The girls at the long tables on the right are using gas irons to press delicate trimmings and garments. The polishing machines on the left had a gas heated cylinder at the back, with an ironing table top controlled by a pedal. The girls could put a fine finish on dress shirts and collars by pushing them under the heated roller by the table top. Two types of collar were polished this way, the every day collars of office workers, solicitors, bank clerks and the like, and winged dress collars.

92. This typical 1914 delivery cart is standing in Doxey Road in front of a fence made from old railway sleepers. The railway trucks in the background are marked C.R.C. (Cannock and Rugely Colliery) and were probably delivering coal to Hall's coal wharf further along the road, from the nearby Cannock Chase coalfields.

93. Life in towns depended upon hay in the years before motor vehicles became common. Horses were kept going largely on hay and vast quantities were needed by town horses. It was not only the horses that drew private carriages but also all the delivery carts, from the large flat drays that distributed goods brought by rail to the small delivery vehicles of milkmen, bakers and grocers. Once hay had been cut it had to be turned so that it dried evenly. Then, while the weather remained fine it was raked together by a horse drag-rake before being loaded by hand onto waggons and taken to be made into stacks. Stafford was as dependent upon hay as other towns and this photograph was taken on a farm at Hixon, a few miles from the town.

94. Lea and Son's Motor House, seen in this photograph, was opened on the Newport Road in 1910. At this date petrol was sold in cans and motorists exchanged their empty cans for full ones at any garage. Petrol pumps had not yet been introduced. This photograph seems to have been taken soon after The Motor House opened. By 1920 The Motor House was still on the same site but the proprietor was A. Greatrex. Greatrex' garage is still here.

95. This early motor-car was made in France and bought, it is said, by the family who lived in Tillington Hall. This was a luxury vehicle for people who were used to riding in a horse-drawn carriage and had a footman who rode outside the car at the back and, whenever it stopped, alighted smartly ready to open the door for one of the passengers. Meanwhile the driver remained in his seat just as the driver of a horse-drawn carriage did. Soon people realised that while the horses could not be left without a hand on the reins, a petrol engine could be left so that the driver could alight and open the door and the footman was made redundant.

96. Above: The railway line crossed the main Lichfield Road at Queensville, at first there was a level crossing, later this was thought to be too dangerous and a bridge was erected over the line. Accidents still happened, however, this picture taken in 1925, is of one of two cars which skidded over the Queensville Bridge embankment, the vehicle hurtled down and came to a stop on the edge of the pond.

Below: In October, 1926, a lorry travelling late at night was forced into the wall of Radford Bridge when another lorry pulled out in front of it. The wall gave way and the vehicle plunged 20 feet into a field by the River Penk. The driver crawled from under the wreckage suffering only from bruises.

97. This view of Bridge Street shows the Picture House with its mock-tudor gable to fit in with the adjoining buildings. When it opened on 23rd February, 1914, it was the third cinema in Stafford and described as 'one of the most up-to-date and luxuriously fitted buildings of its kind, lavishly furnished, with accommodation for 1,000'. The price of seats ranged from three pence to a shilling and a free afternoon cup of tea was served at matinees. From its first silent film – 'The House of Temperley' – the cinema has seen all the major changes of the film industry and remains today outwardly much as it was in 1914: the oldest surviving cinema in the town.

98. Wilmot Martin, born in 1874, was a farmer in Hixon near Stafford. During the First World War he organised concerts to raise funds for the soldiers, and afterwards for St. Dunstans. He was fond of singing Scottish songs, inspired by having heard Harry Lauder, the famous Scottish entertainer, sing at Blackpool. He became friends with the artist who christened Wilmot 'Staffordshire's Harry Lauder'. He raised many hundreds of pounds for charity, dressed as he appears in this postcard.

99. The River Penk and the Staffordshire and Worcestershire Canal run through the fields at Rickerscote. Every Winter, after snow and heavy rain they flooded across from Radford to Silkmore, and the area looked like a vast lake, with herons and seagulls, and sometimes swans, swimming on it. If this expanse froze over, it was fairly safe to skate on, as the water was not too deep. In this picture you can see the local people enjoying skating and sliding on the ice about 1910.

100. Stafford Common is the remnant of the Common land inclosed in 1800. Anyone from Stafford was entitled to graze cows and horses here, horse races were sometimes held and fairs and circuses put up their side-shows here. The Staffordshire Advertiser of December, 1890, reported that 'A Golf Club has just been formed by number of gentlemen at Stafford who have secured the use of the Common for an annual sum, and such slight preparation as the ground requires will be carried out under the direction of a professional player from Hoylake. For some time past the game has been played at Coton Hill Institution where the golf course starts and finishes on the cricket pitch and extends for one and a half miles over adjoining fields. This ancient game is gaining in popularity every day'. This photograph shows the golf course on the Common.

101. Stafford's Siemens Works Morris Men about 1910. This most English of customs has been carried on in Staffordshire for at least 500 years. They wore red and yellow sashes, and knee length trousers called 'hoggers', they carried decorated sticks which had ribbons and bells at the end.

102. The Maternity and Child Welfare Committee of the Corporation organised a Baby Day annually, this photograph was taken in July, 1924. Prizes were awarded for the best decorated prams, and the bonniest baby. A procession of mothers, pushing their decorated prams, wound through the Main Street led by the Borough Military Band, the Mayor and members of the council, it finished in the Victoria Park. Here tea was dispensed and prizes distributed.

103. Staffords first aerial display was in October 1912. Crowds watched Gustav Hamel's monoplane being unloaded at Stafford Station and taken through the streets to Lammascotes where even greater crowds paid one shilling each for admission to the field. About 3,500 people saw Hamel's plane 'bound across the grass and then rise gradually like a great bird', to quote the reporter in the Staffordshire Advertiser. This was only the first of several flights made by Hamel that day. This photograph seems to have been taken as the plane came in to land at the Lammascotes.

104. This group of happy people are the employees and their families of Jackson and Follicks's shop and bakery. They were on their way to Trentham Gardens on a sunny day in 1900.

105. Brocton in the early-twentieth century was a quiet rural village. This postcard published by W.H. Smith & Sons shows the small green in the centre of the village before the First World War.

106. Many village post offices were no more than private houses with a room set aside for post office business. This picturesque thatched house at Walton-on-the-Hill just outside Stafford was photographed about 1910 for William Shaw of Burslem to use as a postcard.

107. Above: Milford is a small hamlet on the edge of that part of Cannock Chase called Milford Common. In the late-nineteenth and early-twentieth century Milford became a popular place for visitors. Special excursion trains ran from Stafford to Milford Station, cyclists found it a not too energetic four mile ride, carriages drove out there on sunny afternoons. The focus of this was the Barley Mow, an old inn that existed as early as 1834 when it was kept by Peggy Auldritt. By 1900 it had been extended to provide for the new visitors.

Below: Milford Common became the favourite spot for a Saturday or Sunday day out in the early-twentieth century. The great influx of visitors attracted a weekend fair with swings, side-shows and donkey rides. This is one of a series of postcards, published by William Shaw of Burslem, which show crowds pouring out of Milford Station and over the railway bridge onto the Common and the crowds on the Common. All were taken on the same day since some children followed the photographer and managed to appear on more than one postcard.

THE DONKEYS ON MILFORD CHASE.

108. Isaac Walton was born in Stafford in 1593. He is best known for his book 'The Complete Angler'. He owned this cottage in Shallowford, near Stafford, where a Walton Museum was set up. In May, 1927, the thatched roof caught fire and before it was extinguished only the outer walls and two chimneys were left standing. Fortunately the contents of the Museum were saved. Eccleshall Fire Brigade tried to put out the fire with water from the Shallowford Brook, which Isaac Walton had once fished. The cottage was restored almost immediately but without a thatched roof.